Love & other Distractions:

A guide to self-love, interpersonal relationships, and anxiety

By Kristin Ariel

Acknowledgments
To my son Kamren and little sister Crystal, I love you, and need you even more than you need me.

TABLE OF CONTENTS

Prologue

"In a room full of darkness you could still be the light of the world"

We are inspired to pursue many things in life but often become discouraged because of distractions such as love, lust, anxiety, social media, and personalization. There are many things we pursue in school, but nothing can prepare us for everything we experience in life; except life itself. A lifelong eagerness to pursue understanding of myself and others asserts that actual parts of this process requires imperfections while being damn near perfect, plus wisdom and insight beyond years. A lifetime of neglect, obsession, and abuse with an intense teenage rollercoaster of popularity, solitude, and non-existence, as well as failed counseling attempts equals more than a few doses of reality which have given me the confidence and security I have today. Throughout these instances I have sustained a unique context of strength, helping me to remain self-assured over and over, even throughout uncontrollable events and circumstances. People sometimes suffer in silence at work, at home, and in the general public, as well as around friends and family. I learned how to love myself at a young age and fall in love with myself over and over again as an adult. If there was a Ph.D. in life experience-I would have it.
This is how I put myself back together.

Mantra for females:

I am beautiful.
I am strong.
I am intelligent.
I am balanced.
I am a light.
I am a beautiful, strong, intelligent, balanced light.

Mantra for males:

I know I am capable.
I can maintain my strength.
I am worthy of appreciation before, during, and after success.
I am capable and worthy of maintaining my strength no
matter the timetable or circumstance of my success.

Mantra for anxiety:

I am ok.
It's almost over.
And when it's over
I am still true to myself.
I am not lacking within.
I am okay because after the anxiety is over I know who I am,
not ever lacking because anxiety could affect anyone.

Chapter One: Heartbreak

(the past)

Heartbreak

Heartbreaks are always in our past because, even if you are experiencing heartbreak right now-your heart is already broken. Some believe you can die from a broken heart; however, you can always at least attempt to heal your heart if you make a choice to keep living. Past heartbreaks teach us about new heartbreaks, although nothing can prepare you for true heartbreak. We have an idea of what a broken heart feels like before it happens, but the extent of the actual pain is unpredictable and sometimes unimaginable. A minor heartbreak could result from a casual friendship that turned intimate and never repaired itself, while a major heartbreak could be an infatuation confused for healthy expectations. We are unintentionally attracted to and intentionally invested in each person we truly fall in love or lust with.

Some people gain an ego boost from intentionally hurting someone else. Completely aware of the person's feelings for them, they take advantage of their desires and capitalize on their vulnerability. These people are usually unable to provide an ego boost to themselves, likely never recovering from past rejection and heartbreak of their own. These are traumatic experiences that remain within a person throughout adulthood since childhood. Additionally, there are people who are emotionally incapacitated-whenever someone hurts them they hurt themselves. Hurting yourself because of how someone else feels about you is the ultimate pain and an unhealthy choice.

The Logic of Heartbreak

Heartbreak occurs when our expectations in love are not met. However, just because someone breaks our heart does not mean they do *not* love us. It does not mean they *never* loved us, and it does not mean they will not *continue* loving us. Some of us know this already because we have hurt someone we love, even more than once; if it is possible for us, it is possible for someone else. True love is not a complete wash; its characteristics are full of possibilities and extremities. Heartbreak is largely applied to love but also pertains to friends and especially family. A popular cliché says family is capable of hurting us the most, but this is unrealistic because it is the result of our own expectations we place onto them. Heartbreak is almost inevitable-to get hurt is to be open to love. We are all capable of being hurt. Anyone can experience heartbreak that no amount of money, confidence, or prestige can barricade. Attempting to understand why someone does *not* love you is an inappropriate, unhealthy way of thinking that does not justify you being hurt, nor create a need for you to make unwarranted or unnecessary changes to gain love.

Healing

It's easier to love someone than it is trying not to love someone. Sometimes, the more you love people the less you love yourself. Sometimes, the more you love someone the less you like yourself, because either you are aware how unstandardized it is for you to be in such a compromising position or you acknowledge that the love you are giving is undeserved. What is important is that you love yourself in case someone stops loving you. What if no one loved you? It is extreme but in the midst of our emotions we feel extremities. Love yourself more than you ever loved anyone else. You cannot allow heartbreak to leave you broken; you can be fully aware of the pain without allowing it to break you. Realize when things hurt, things take time. We often get overly hopeful or overly sad (two extremes). The preceding is a setup for disappointment because we tend to want instant or magical and radical change and answers. When this does not happen we get discouraged.

In the beginning of your own personal growth and healing, you may have to learn to love yourself over and over again. If you are forced to accept that you love someone, at least love them in personal strength and confidence. If you love someone in weakness- you are already hurting yourself before the other person has the opportunity to. Some people are afraid of walking away, due to extreme vulnerability and emotional attachment. There are four different types of attachment; anxious-preoccupied, dismissive-avoidant, secure, & fearful avoidant, and all are healthy. It is the person we are attached *to* that determines the effectiveness or the failure of our attachment to them. Instead of being afraid to walk away-be afraid of *not* being able to walk away; because of not loving yourself, not believing in your own optimism, not understanding your self-worth, and not having faith in your own expectations for yourself.

"Know your worth, then add tax!"-Chanel CoCo

Being strong is painful but it can alternatively feel so good, because that's when you are loving or learning to love yourself the most, or both. Being strong on your own could mean the possibility of receiving nothing from someone else, and walking away from someone could mean them never loving you again. This could also determine or falsely determine whether they loved you at all. If they never make an effort again after you walk away, it is possible they never loved you enough or never loved you at all. One thing is for sure-

"You must protect your inner peace at all costs!" –Jackie Olayiwonola Aina

Whether someone loves you or does not- you must make a personal choice to love yourself. This would involve healthy thinking, attempts at happiness anyway, and considering yourself first. You may never know if a person loves you or not-will you give up on yourself forever? The moment you begin thinking of yourself as less without someone you are breaking your own heart. People are meant to add to your life, not deplete from it.

Love in general can be full of questions, false hope, and turmoil. Sometimes, the answers to our questions in love can be found in closure. Part of healing is not force, and part of closure involves conclusions. We are forced to draw conclusions when we don't get the answers we are seeking, because we cannot force the person to respond, react, or even love us.

Closure

Closure may seem imminent and required when we are in a state of pain and desperation. It can bring an end that we are unprepared for, amongst an inability to cope and or move forward. When we bring closure to a situation it does not necessarily mean we are ready to heal. Healing only comes with time.

Closure could mean an unexpected end or an amicable end to something brief or long-term, healthy or unhealthy, painful or just plain content. It can be forgiving, and is similar to forgiveness in accordance with its healing potential. Just like in forgiveness, closure requires a person to come to terms with a situation.

"Sometimes wanting someone isn't enough. Sometimes you have to choose yourself" –r.h. Sin

What to Do

There are two ways to bring closure. One form of closure could be an amicable end, such as contacting the person to attempt to end on a positive note. You may for the person to only remember good things about you, without a negative perspective regarding you by acknowledging your maturity at any time in the future. Your courteous effort, however, does not guarantee empathy. The other form of closure could be not contacting the person at all, as well as never again responding to efforts on their part. The main reason for closure would be acknowledging your feelings-be it anger, sadness, as well as respectfully providing the opportunity for the other person to communicate about their feelings towards you or the situation as well. One important thing to also remember is closure does not require a circumstance to return to normalcy; closure is often an end.

The Logic of Closure

The not-so-healthy aspect of heartbreak features two extreme responses: overly accepting heartbreak or not accepting heartbreak at all. Someone who refutes heartbreak could be intimidatingly independent, cold, and detached. Instead of coming to terms with their feelings they choose not acknowledge they have feelings about the situation at all, never contacting the person again and never responding. This is a classic case of shutting down-when someone is so dependent upon their personal strength and survival they forfeit their own feelings, possibly from pride. The latter of not accepting heartbreak at all is due to abnormal attachment; the inability to separate the love for themselves from their love for the other person. Because of the intense emotional attachment they have formed, it is nearly impossible to survive without the other person; it could take years to overcome the heartbreak and could possibly turn into obsession.

For anyone, heartbreak is a difficult event to cope with and not be affected by. It would be unrealistic not to think of someone you shared feelings or intimacy with, or someone you claim not to love anymore, even after you've moved on with someone else. Why? Because we are humans who operate on emotions involuntarily, whether we embrace them or deny them. Ideally, there should be a balance between the two; you should be able to acknowledge your feelings while also being capable of moving on. Do not overwhelm yourself about a love that is uncertain. If we have to force it or make it love us-we should not pursue it. We naturally cannot help if we want it, but forced love is not real love.

*A study of 6,000 at Binghampton University New York and University College London found that men had a harder time healing from heartbreak and never fully recover but "just move on, while women reported higher levels of emotional and physical pain but recover stronger and more completely overall.

Chapter Two: Forgiveness

(moving forward)

Forgiveness

Society tends to teach us that there is a good and evil; rarely a middle ground or grey area. This black and white perspective is a paradigm that teaches us not even to forgive ourselves, labeling ourselves as "all bad" or "all good". We've seen society model this perspective, especially in the media. For example; a cheater is not forgiven because a partner considers the cheating 'retroactive'-a wash of the person's entire character. Reality needs to be considered, evaluating a new type of realistic forgiveness. Upon considering forgiveness of someone, a ton of characteristics should be evaluated-a person's background, their coping skills, their capabilities and potential, as well as achievements and all of the positive things about them. In reference to their coping skills, we highlight their response to stress-how they deal with stress and how they react to it. A good example of this is addiction; addictions are double edged swords that people rely on for stress relief that actually cause more stress, such as compulsive gambling, drinking, cheating, and drug use. We know from general wisdom that forgiveness is for us and not the other person involved. The truth in this cliché asserts that if you first do not forgive someone personally it could directly affect your own character. You could subconsciously or intentionally harbor anger, hatred, and worry amongst other negative emotions associated with not moving forward. A spiritual person should be aware that not forgiving could block blessings and positivity, sending negative energies to your life/universe. Forgiveness, if done right, should be a positive experience, or burden releasing, for we know that positive experiences lead to overall hopefulness.

Not forgiving others is still an action; it is excessive, no matter the severity of the situation because forgiveness is for ourselves, not the struggle of projecting our feelings onto others. Everyone who desires a second chance deserves one. In this lies the complexity of genuineness, however, this is not debatable as long as the second chance given is not according to the guilty's terms. A person has the right to forgive according to their own terms, so long as it is healthy and appropriate for themselves. In reference to second chances, we have to allow people a chance to change and grow, which motivates and inspires them to believe in growth so that they would want to keep changing for the better.

Everyone is at least capable of desiring change, regardless of their ability to actually change. A narcissist, or someone who is intentionally unrealistic about their behaviors, how they affect others, and does not take accountability would be a perfect candidate for no forgiveness, as sincerity tends to enable their personalities; however, we are not in a position to determine who deserves forgiveness as it is not based upon others. The murderer, the cheater, the liar, the thief-let's assume everyone deserves forgiveness, because the possibility of sincerity and goodness in someone's heart is more important than ten thousand instances of people who actually do not deserve forgiveness (the constitution is actually set up this way, to allow the guilty go free under reasonable doubt at the expense of hopes in not punishing the innocent). You would not want to miss out on giving someone a second chance when they truly needed it and were capable of fulfilling it! Remember you do not have to compromise yourself to forgive, because forgiveness does not always mean reconciliation, as it is not a requirement for forgiveness.

Chapter Three: Anxiety

(being okay)

Anxiety

Anxiety is the new silent fear. The quiet suffering that plagues heart rates and thoughts, affecting 40 million adults between the ages of 18 to 54 (NIMH, 2016). Anxiety does not originate from low self-esteem, but can affect it. Characterized by panic, it can surge with an increase in peer pressure and expectations. People with anxiety can generally be identified by fidgety behavior or any nervousness during events that typically require an amount of patience; from waiting in line at the local grocery to posing for pictures with friends. There is a normal spectrum of anxiety that would involve typical worries, such as public speaking or waiting on a reply from a lover before going to sleep at night. P

eople who suffer from anxiety are prone to overreacting, becoming easily frustrated; being hypersensitive, as well as overcompensating for the way others make them feel. Overcompensation might involve being over-celebratory, euphoria, or extreme pessimism in fear of failing. It's possible people who are anxious also fear judgment where there is none, misplacing anger as well. Sometimes, because we are living in a state of anxiousness, the only person treating you different is you. In life, there will be situations and general 'rough days' that are inevitable and unavoidable; the key is to be as resilient as possible.

There is one major key to anxiety-you're not perfect. No matter what you do or say. You *will* mess up, there *will* be days more stressful than others, but there is nothing you can do to be perfect. Anxiety often stems from two components-us trying to control everything, and the fearful realization that we *cannot* control everything. Everything is not going to be perfect all of the time; therefore, you are not going to be perfect all of the time. Leave room for yourself to make human error, be open to humor, and accept criticism.

Often we think that others have an easier, worry free life while we suffer; this is untrue as celebrities suffer from anxiety the same. The only difference is the resources that may be available to celebrities, such as money, high levels of therapy, and medication. Therapy, medication, and some sponsorship are available to everyone and could help, though there is no cure for anxiety itself.

During obviously dangerous situations, of course, our anxiety may 'soar through the roof'. However, in safe daily environments when your mind is in a state of panic, you have to remind it that everything is okay and that nothing horrendous is occurring at the moment. The overanalyzing and overthinking components of anxiety are also excessive and stressful to the human mind.

"It's not always just the heart-sometimes the mind breaks as well" –r.h. Sin

Anxiety is like feeling alone. In a room full of people you feel panic and no one is aware, no one else is experiencing it, and because no one notices your panic- no one knows to help. You could feel threatened suddenly and everyone around you appears to feel safe. During these intense circumstances or, because of them, it's normal to feel like isolating yourself. However, while isolation may temporarily make you feel safer, it still causes feelings of loneliness all over again, like a double-edged sword.

Loneliness

Being lonely doesn't deem you abnormal, unattractive, or even unhappy. There is an obvious difference between independence and loneliness. Some people are happy being independent and self-sufficient, opting to be lonely and may have grown accustomed to it. They are clear about their wants and do not wish to compromise in any circumstance, such as a relationship. They feel very capable with or without someone. There are those who have not opted to be independent and wish for a companion, and so they feel underestimated in a state of loneliness. However, a relationship does not guarantee freedom from loneliness. Someone could be a component of a relationship and still feel lonely, or not be in a relationship and still feel loved or fulfilled. Not even fame is a freedom from loneliness.

Anxiety can cause feelings of tension at all times, or feelings of defensiveness without provocation or identification. Because of anxiety, many times we place even more pressure on ourselves thinking we have to do something; something to change people, to change the situation, or make ourselves feel better. For example, waiting for a reply from someone we love can make us feel tense and cause our level of anxiety to rise, knowing we cannot exert a quicker response without overreacting or drastic measures.

What to Do

Because there is no cure for anxiety we must train ourselves not to panic. Sometimes if we just be 'still' or quiet, doing nothing sometimes actually changes the situation. If doing nothing doesn't change the situation, however, at least it prohibits doing something drastic, overreacting, or not creating additional stress. "Calm" is a wonderful word that can be used as a mantra, like a reminder-giving *calm* responses, thinking *calmly*, and behaving *calmly* can help both manage and reject anxiety.

What Not to Do/Things to Avoid

Darkness

Living with anxiety is like living under a dark cloud. It can be depressing, hindering, and full of extreme pessimism. Some people suffer from anxiety so much so that they begin behaviors such as retreating to their home to avoid the public and crowds. It can become a habit to isolate ourselves inside with curtains drawn; letting no sunlight in as a metaphor to the positivity we withdraw ourselves from. Nyctophiliacs are those who enjoy darkness and the night, while some individuals who suffer from Body Dysmorphic Disorder perform daily activities, such as hygiene, in the darkness to avoid the burden of viewing themselves in the mirror. If not careful, darkness could become a part of everyday life for people who are already struggling with emotional or mental darkness.

Some environments themselves are dark matter. Spiritual individuals might say any place can be full of negative spirits. A stressful home or a draining job-any environment that forces you to be in a daily intensity of pressure, negativity, or judgment that you are ill-equipped to keep sustaining in is darkness. Exhausting all possible options is best before continuing this way of life.

What to Do

If not already required by career or family demands, attempt to wake up early and open all curtains and blinds, letting in as much sunlight as possible to combat the subconscious thoughts of darkness. Making an effort to prepare for the day allows us the attitude of positivity, hopefulness, and joy we should expect in the hours to come. Turning on lamps and lighting candles at night helps to still keep a positive and light atmosphere at night, while simultaneously soothing and relaxing.

Alcohol

Alcohol resembles two layers. Consciously, or on the surface layer, alcohol is a sweet escape to life's problems; a metaphoric smooth jazz that relaxes us, making us temporarily feel calmer, better, and more intuitive. Anxiety is already a feeling of darkness, so alcohol only influences this feeling even though we seek alcohol to feel better. Subconsciously, alcohol to anxiety is like a double-edged sword, just as isolation is to anxiety. On levels of happiness, alcohol makes you feel low, though you drink it to feel high. Some people become so impressed with the way alcohol eases their anxiety that they begin to consume it more regularly – this is known as *self-medicating,* and people who suffer from anxiety are three times more likely to turn to substance abuse than those who do not have such symptoms (Alcohol Rehab, 2016).

What to Do

Rather than using alcohol as an escape to anxiety, acknowledge the possibility of an alcohol addiction or the potential for one in the future. Look for other forms of temporary happiness, such as favorite juices, smoothies, or fruits. Unhealthy foods and sweets and retail therapies are common misrepresentations of alternatives to unhealthy choices that should not be sought regularly. Daily multivitamins are severely underrated, as new supplements contain mood stimulants and appetite suppressants, improving overall health while increasing metabolism to combat feelings of sluggishness.

Loud and Crowded Environments

People are everywhere. Still, those with anxiety struggle to feel normal in public and contemplate avoiding people. Many may feel that parties, raves, carnivals, and environments that elicit fun are healthy for people who experience anxiety and loneliness. However, for some people, the more people there are the lonelier they feel. Loud or crowded environments can be an overwhelming of stimuli for people who suffer from anxiety, creating more stress. Overwhelming atmospheres could include hyperactive or horse playing kids, energetic animals, or even the less than typical amount of people we are unfamiliar with. For those who are already prone to hypersensitivity, crowds and loud environments can be almost suffocating, and panic more prone to onset. Some people just genuinely dislike large crowds or loud noises and environments, which is okay.

What to Do

Don't look for stress. Many times we are so accustomed to being in a state of worry that we feel abnormal in a state of happiness. We have a subconscious tendency to try and remember what is stressful for us. The attempt should be getting out of the state of worry and knowing who you are as an individual, even in a crowd.

Making a conscious effort to do typical activities in the general public as opposed to avoiding the general public is sufficient. Within home environments, noise from televisions and radios, etc., can be kept at minimal level. A frequent driver might find solace in sacrificing their normal pop radio station for a healing or meditation podcast.

Chapter Four: Distractions

(they're everywhere)

Distractions

In our daily lives, there are distractions everywhere. Many distractions can be considered both positive and negative, even the negative distractions being inspiring and motivational. It is our personal responsibility and discretion to distinguish between those distractions which are inspiring to us or not worth the demand and sacrifice. Our tolerance varies individually, and so does our aspirations for the future. Anything that is not beneficial to our future is typically not fruitful and is liable to sacrifice.

YOUR JOB as a distraction

There are many interpersonal relationships associated with jobs. On a spectrum that includes being overly friendly or being extremely reserved, some form of balance between these extremes is ideal in order to maintain a healthy amount of respect and professionalism in the workplace. After all, your reputation is at stake. Typically we spend more time at our jobs than at home, regardless if we enjoy our workplace or coworkers. Aside from entrepreneurs, business owners, or any leadership role, we do not get the pleasure of choosing our colleagues and, if we did, the selection of coworkers would be better tailored to our personalities and morals. Therefore, it is unlikely we would like or care for every individual we work with. It is ideal that every workplace be professional, punctual, organized, beneficial, and respectful, however, that ideology is sometimes far from the truth and unrealistic. In today's society where morals have changed, employees feel more entitled to a job role rather than eager to perform it, especially if it is not of public service. Hospitality and teamwork in the work place is sometimes replaced with atmospheric envy, profanity, laziness, and zero accountability. Some people are assholes no matter where they go, and can't keep their disdain and rage from polluting even the most peaceful, warm, and loving places (Breggin, 2014). The same negativity that exists outside of a professional environment can and does exist within one.

How to Function at Work

Being harmonious in the workplace will require the maintenance of many arms-distance relationships with colleagues. The routine greetings and farewells are courteous and respectful; because it symbolizes that you acknowledge others other than yourself. Every workplace requires a team of individuals; therefore, some companies require or favor that you know how to be a part of a team. Individually we do not know everything, but together many people contribute in many ways. Thus others are capable of learning, helping, and sustaining one another.

Personal business such as basic marital status, educational accolades, age, and kids is appropriate for sharing in the workplace, and virtually could be summed up in less than five minutes. A brief synopsis about family you created and your accomplishments gives people a small glimpse into who you are, and is enough to earn the typical respect required. It is ideal that respect be automatically given in the workplace but it is unrealistic, as it is even harder for people to respect you if they do not know or understand you. Furthermore, the sharing of intimate details with colleagues, such as previous failures, infidelities, innocent or intentional crushes, and fears are inappropriate. Given the opportunity or upon the termination of a workplace friendship or employment in general, personal details could become public business, or used in an attempt to harm you or advance someone else, or both. Within the workplace we still remain individuals, so physical dress or appearance is our own personal choice and the responsibility of the employer to uphold or not uphold.

Personal privacy in the workplace is also a personal choice, and its consequences are the responsibility of the person who is sharing. There is a false theory that insinuates gossip exists in every job-it does not. We know this to be false because of loving family businesses, entrepreneurships and motivated partnerships, and general work environments where employees genuinely succeed and help each other. Workplace gossip often exists as an escape and excuse for those who have grown tired of their job positions, are unhappy in their personal lives, or simply have the tendency to envy others. Just as genuine concern exists so does fake concern, as we are not always aware of who has our best interest at heart even outside of work; therefore we should strive to maintain a positive, private, professional image in the workplace, without inflicting the stress and negativity of work at home on the people we genuinely love.

LOVE as a distraction

It is very appealing and subconsciously tempting to try to make someone love you; even writhing your heart trying to discover whether someone loves you or not is tempting. We are all worthy of love and need love, but today's relationship trends tend to follow a path of emotionless, commitment-lacking, non-attachment that deceives us into thinking that seeking love is a sign of insecurity. If someone loves you-that's great, however-additionally you need to be everything you can be in case they do not truly love you, stop loving you, or fall out of love with you. Even the healthiest of couples are capable of growing apart or falling apart-be it over time or in an irreversible instant. The one thing that remains or is constant throughout any scenarios mentioned is love. Love is true, real, and genuine, and cannot be avoided, turned off, or ignored.

Loving someone is easy but can be hard, and love not reciprocated is hell on earth. It is our responsibility to show people how to love us, and how to treat us. The people that seem to automatically know what we need-those are typically the people we marry. However, even the most perfect candidates to our hearts bestow flaws and have their own personal issues.

There are three associations with love that should be acknowledged: limerence, love, and lust.

Love

True love may still require you to allow someone to love you and let you go. Whether they know they cannot provide you with your needs, or they have their own standard of needs that must be met. Naturally, we may not be able to meet the needs of someone we love every time, but if needs are not met the majority of the time or the effort itself is non-existent, the love is invalid. Love is not a choice but within love there are choices.

If you find happiness, or know how to be effective, in your individuality-you make it easier for someone else to love you, want you, and work for you; in addition to successfully getting you, having you, and keeping you.

A huge misconception about love is that no one can love you if you do not love yourself. The actual fact is that it takes a genuine, mature person to love and accept you no matter your insecurities and join you on your journey to learning to love yourself. Within the misconception lies another fact-if you love yourself it makes it easier to accept the appropriate love from someone else. Respect for yourself would force you to choose to be happy or terminate a pattern of unhappiness within a relationship, or terminate an unhealthy or unhappy relationship overall. Also, manipulative and deceiving persons can easily recognize someone who does not love themselves and cause harm or heartbreak.

Lust

Lust is love in euphoric and temporary form. Its characteristics could involve instant connection, deception, risks, and manipulation. The passion of lust can be overwhelming and feel certain, causing an addiction or habit. The absence of giving title to a lustful interaction or relationship can be both intriguing and confusing, causing persons to be misled often. Lust is not love because where in love there is genuine concern and sacrifices for the future, there is none in lust, and substance is lacking. A candidate for lust is unlikely a candidate for the future because of incapabilities, such as the ability to be honest, sustainable, secure, and assured the attraction is unlikely to withstand the tests of time, patience, and loyalty.

Unless two people agree on the absence of obligation and commitment to one another, lust is still temporary because of its design of emotionless animation that plays out into disappointment based upon the irony of feelings. One misconception of lust is the vacancy of expectations; even in a lustful interaction there are expectations of nonjudgment, risk-taking, and confidentiality.

Limerence

Limerence is lust characterized by more obsession than addiction. The same euphoric attributes of lust exist in limerence but are amplified by control or, and intense anger ensues from the lack there of. The extreme desire to control someone or extreme unemotional attachment to someone you do not love is limerence. An attachment to someone who is harmful or hurtful to you is most likely love, which an attachment to someone you consciously hurt or harm is considered limerence. Limerence is a form of lust that requires us to focus so much on the healthy attributes that the extremely unhealthy attributes are not ignored but still have no bearing in our discretion. Being vulnerable is a component of love, but being vulnerable to the point of being victimized-be it self-inflicting with no reaction from the other party-is unbecoming.

"In some relationships people are miserable apart but together it's so hard" –Sevyn Streeter

SOCIAL MEDIA as a distraction

If you seek validation on social media, you will experience an infinite rollercoaster of approval, disapproval, and basic lack of concern. As a society, we admire celebrities and look to social media for the sharing of valuable memories and priorities because we find it reveling and positive. The same mixed opinions that exist in society also exist on social media. In a world of intense politics and biased media portrayals, it can be hard to value social media or even participate online. These perspectives are no paradigm for the average person, as they include a disproportionate mix of justice and injustice, optimism and pessimism that have been added to cyber form. When we engage in social media we are subconsciously comparing our lives to others. We know this because at times we log out of our social media accounts feeling "down" or worth less. The trend created by pictures that portray happiness and romance causes us to envy, both voluntarily and involuntarily, because it suggests that others' lives are more rewarding than ours. Often we close our social media accounts feeling more determined and inspired to dress better, exercise more frequently, buy and spend more, or look better because of our subconscious responses to what we perceive on the internet.

Celebrities

Celebrities are not required to be saviors nor should be deemed villains to the public, as neither extreme is morally accurate, though professionally they adhere to higher standards. It seems as society fails to consider celebrities as peers, leaving little room for them to make human error. Celebrities can be faced with the same emotional and physical objections as any other infamous person.

A celebrity, by logical definition, is someone deemed popular amongst or by others; therefore, anyone you feel is important to you is a celebrity, as well as anyone you do not consider personally valuable does not have to be celebrated by you. In this millennium, the media tends to decide for us who is a celebrity and who is not, however, anyone who makes national headlines is generally considered famous or can achieve fame. Remember, the media shows favor, and as a society we tend to let the media decide who is deserving of it and who is not, while none of us are undeserving of favor as we are all worthy in some way. Also, the priorities portrayed on social media by celebrities are extremely skewed because of socioeconomic status differences. But to prohibit celebrities from failures and disappointments and to depend on social media for morals and values is absurd.

Privacy

Personal privacy has been a thing of the past since social media networks began evolving. Facebook®, Instagram®, and Snapchat®, to name a few, require us to divulge a considerable amount of our lives to others. Now, according to society, people who are private online are considered unpopular and leading a boring life, and non-inspirational to others. How much we share socially should always be an individual discretion.

Those who post their relationships via social media, be it words of gratefulness or bliss or pictures portraying happiness and fun, are not necessarily living their life as such. In other words, everything portrayed on social media is not so. Happiness, financial wealth, security, religious and spiritual faith, etc. continue to vary in the lives of people outside of social media. Everything misportrayed in reality is also misportrayed online. In the same fashion, absence on social media does not equal the absence of comfort, security, confidence, happiness, success, romance, and support. We tend to heavily misjudge others online, including extreme inspiration and extreme despair, while privacy is still a personal choice.

What to Do

On social media we subconsciously perceive, just as in reality. The reality is there are many attempts to impress those whom are secretly miserable themselves. Because we lack the ability to always distinguish what is honest or what is fabricated online, you should establish your own brand online. Choose your own level of privacy, which talents you wish to display, a frequency trend of how active you are and how much you post, and limit your posts to what is important to you personally. If you value your character online, try to limit your posts to positivity only, nothing negative.

MUSIC as a distraction

Listening to Rihanna does not crown you a 'savage', and listening to Willie Nelson does not hail you a 'stoner'. Music is multifaceted for everyone; its inspiration or comfort changing by atmosphere or circumstance. Almost always, music can be just a *simple distraction*; helping to pass time as its white noise fades the typical and subconscious daily worries. It can be a heartfelt enthusiasm, inspiring a jump into the day, air, or errands and encouraging a joyful state of mind about life and the present. And finally, music can be soul-excruciating, wrenching us into a reminiscence of happiness at the expense of pain from a disappointment or heartache. While all genres are composed of sad songs, Rhythm and Blues or, R&B, and Country music tend to carry the torch for heartbreak music. Subconsciously, music affects us all. One instance of enjoying a pop hit can unknowingly and quickly turn into a crying session. The memories of fun could be audibly paralyzing or the following song could instantly inflict thoughts and emotions of turmoil. A Christian rock band could save someone's soul in worship while their family experiences hail gospel as praise music Rap music, along with Hip-Hop, is either an escape from daily socioeconomic struggles or a celebration of newfound wealth.

Consciously, music causes us to respond in different ways. Trap music, for example, can inspire some to rob someone of their wealth or inspire them to acquire their own. Where country music is alcohol-persuasive over heartache, it can persuade some to break someone else's heart in revenge. Because music is so multi-faceted it can only be labeled or categorized in genre, not action.

Mental capacities at the time of listening play an important role in music. Because we all mentally and emotionally respond to music differently, our ability to cope and level of stress in correlation with music varies. People who tend to "bottle everything in" may be unable to do so in regards to music, and people who "wear their heart on their sleeve" may be able to muster a sad love song or two, and vice versa. We respond to music according to our individuality, which involves our personal experiences. By now we know that particular songs can lead even the strongest or unemotional individual into a convulsion because of its association with circumstances such as death, divorce, or some other despair.

How to Respond to Music / What to Do

We should behave with music according to our strengths. Identifying your weaknesses in music could also help you avoid further emotional or spiritual damage. If we revel in a particular genre and use it for solace and inspiration-that is positive and uplifting, and if we seek refuge in music for heartbreak that is soothing. However, we stunt our own healing when we are distracted by music to the extent that it is non-motivational and hindering to our emotional health. If we know we are unlikely to recover from a music session without being hungover, absent from work, or hopeless then we probably should not engage in that genre until we are able to listen and enjoy with a healthy amount of vigor. Logically, listening to Pharrell's nationally nominated and award-winning song "Happy" does not guarantee happiness, but it does encourage even the coldest of people to ponder something cheerful.

Chapter Five: Perception & Personalization

(understanding)

Perception and Personalization

In life, we experience difficult circumstances and negative things affect us all, but how we perceive it is most important. Our perception, especially about ourselves, is everything. It could take a million things to rattle someone or not rattle someone at all, or it could take just one small thing to send someone else 'over the edge'. Everyone is different; as people's tolerances vary so does the way they handle things. How we handle life is also important.

Your Reaction

In both hindsight and insight, there is no such thing as embarrassment-there is no one person's opinion that exists that is important. We are all equal, sol if it's anyone opinion we value more than our own that is a personal choice. Embarrassment could be considered a normal part of life, not a stressful circumstance, because things do not always happen perfectly. The theory of embarrassment is now debatable.

The "Trip and Fall"

Walking through a crowd you trip and fall on your face. There are many ways you can react to this error. Self-assurance reminds you that you are in the most powerful position, as this error is your own. No matter what, if you do not panic others would find have difficulty panicking in response to you. If others laughed and you remained calm and indifferent, others may find it difficult to continue laughing. You could get upset about others laughing, but you cannot control them; *the sooner they realize you have no interest in trying to control them the importance of the situation is diminished.* Lastly, you could personalize your own trip and fall by panicking, but that would be raising your own anxiety. An emotional, or OCD, or perfectionist might consider their trip and fall the ultimate doom of their entire day, week, or life.

Your reaction to people and circumstances is very important and depends on you. A fragile people who are aware of their tendency to overexert themselves should, in tough situations, make it a habit to behave calmly. Rushing or speeding things out of frustration only creates more room for error, more risks, and increases stress. Adrenaline can motivate the right person or wreak havoc for the wrong person. Often we use expressions such as "He or She made me mad" or "He or She hurt me". These expressions are false, as well as the cliché that "there's no such thing as someone making you do anything". It is true that people and circumstances cause us to feel feelings, such as anger, sadness, pain, and stress; however, it is your reaction that is your complete responsibility. Understandably, it is difficult to manage your responsibility of yourself when faced with daily tensions and oppressions, but in society we are still expected to maintain our characters.

Your reaction, just like your attitude, can dictate the other party's response also, or the position they find themselves in following your reaction. For example, if you panic, it is more than likely others will panic too. Not panicking would not mean lack of fear, just as not elevating your voice would not mean lack of anger. The premise is that if you are less likely to elicit an escalated reaction than you are less likely to receive as escalated response.

Personalization

You must maintain a secure level of self-confidence no matter what happens to you, no matter others' perception of you. People who do not interact with you personally do not know you! This includes an "occasional basis", and is true at your job, your school, etc. When we allow people to know us we are open to their thoughts and opinions, and they are open to ours. When you allow people to declare that they know you you're also allowing them to make any assumptions about you. In making these assumptions people tend to feel their opinions and judgements about you have relevance. This is false. When people such as friends know us they will have a perspective about us that is based upon mostly positivity, more than any other fault or flaw of ours. People who don't know you will be unlikely and unable to state both the positive and negative attributes of you. This is why we cannot give emotional power to people who do not know us or do not "like" us.

You should never mistreat yourself based upon how someone else treats you or feels about you. Getting hurt does not necessarily mean there is something wrong with you. Though you could be an issue, the other party may be an issue also, more than you, or equally. Concerning others' opinions about you-do not adopt them as your own. You should never have to abandon your own self-value as a sacrifice to someone else's peace. Everyone is responsible for their own peace, and giving people your energy is like allowing people into your peace; therefore, be careful to whom you give your energy to. Self-preservation may cause you to forego things and people you thought you loved and needed to maintain your peace. Concerning your circumstances-where you are does not define who you are, if you do not want it to. This is in reference to any success that takes time.

Even selfish individuals have a right to be selfish-their choices and way of life are their responsibility, and so are their consequences. However, they should not pair themselves or surround themselves with selfless people. We all must learn from our own experiences-for us to care enough, want change, and want to understand. This is why self-experiences are sometimes the only way people learn. Their desire to learn must be present.

So many times we take on our circumstances; we grow accustomed to personalizing rough days that are inevitable. We know with certainty that rough days are inevitable and non-selective because even the richest or most famous have bad days. Even the richest and most famous feel lonely and sad. Just as we should not personalize other people's attitudes towards us, we should not personalize our own circumstances in life. Anyone is susceptible to pain, fear, loneliness, and any other feeling of dread. We know this concept is true because there are popular people who are incarcerated or intelligent people who are unemployed or wealthy people who are homeless. We do not have to personalize our jobs, our shelters, our families, etc. We are individually entitled to our own values, self-worth, and aspirations; you can choose to aspire whenever you want! We only need to stay true to ourselves.

Doubt

Aside from hurting you, people will doubt you; however, their doubt is not your responsibility. What is important is that you believe in yourself in the event people doubt you. There may be times when you are the only one believing in you. People will set low standards for you in their conscience without your permission, and for many reasons. People who do not consider themselves special tend to be unable to understand someone else's uniqueness or intentionally refuse to consider it, or over-celebrate others they personally consider special. When you overachieve, the same individuals and others may be in shock. Shock as a response to someone's success should be considered an insult-we should never underestimate anyone. People subconsciously underestimate each other's capabilities. Maybe during your entire acquaintance with someone they have doubted you-your potential, your ambition-without you being aware, maybe even through love they have for you. Some people who wish for personal glory are just not personally willing to make the effort and perform in order to make it happen for themselves. On the other hand, it's easier for people who do not know you to doubt you, so do not take doubt personal.

Envy

Nothing that someone else does can stop another individual from doing what they wish to do. Many religions would contend that whatever is meant for one person is inevitable. Envy stems from the judgement and, often, misjudgment of others. It is sometimes subconsciously existent or inflicted. Envy is severely desensitized in society, especially in the media, in the workplace, and in religious settings. When we acknowledge that envy exists we acknowledge the reality of our success not be accepted by everyone, our notions of negativity or uneasiness being misperceived, and the possibility of both disdain equally to praise in even the safest scenarios.

Perception

How you perceive yourself is of most value and paramount. How others perceive you could be drastically different than how you perceive yourself. Most significantly, out of everyone, you should have the best perception of yourself. You may not be for everyone. People who are aware of you, knowing who you are but are unable to consider you a friend (be it their choice or yours) are speculators. Even individuals who were once close to you-their perception is no longer valid as we as people change and make improvements everyday. Whoever knows you presently; all of your current efforts, aspirations, and your latest thoughts and feelings that you convey to them, know you.

There are two types of people surrounding you and all of them know you are special: people who know you are special and love you for it, and people who know you are special and envy or dislike you for it. In both instances intimidation can circulate. Typically, people who are insecure are intimidated, regardless if they choose. Intimidation is not a personal choice, it is a feeling, but choosing not to be intimidated is. Some will want you to be like everyone else-maybe they will not want you to be or feel special.

When people don't understand you it may cause them to react in many ways. They will assume things about you while they have little to no information concerning you, because they are subconsciously desperate to draw conclusions about you. People could also attempt to outcast you though you never sought a position in their life. The reason for some of these erratic misconceptions is because people struggle with accepting you if you don't attempt their idealizations about what you should be. Even at the lowest parts of your life people will think that's where you belong or that's who you are, even some family and friends.

It's not ever about what others say about you, it's about what you say and think about yourself. If you don't attempt to escape the perceptions and opinions of others, you will forever be indebted to a state of worry. Expectations from others do motivate us, however, our expectations for and from ourselves should be the highest standard of all.

Chapter Six: Your Relationship with You

(feeling better)

Your Relationship with You

The key to your relationship with yourself is liking yourself and knowing yourself. Not only should you be your favorite person, you should also find yourself loving yourself more and more everyday, and trying to be better than you ever were before. When you put yourself first it is transparent, and it will be hard for others to mistreat you. The way we subconsciously treat ourselves is astounding. Often we don't allow ourselves enough time, cheating ourselves out of patience. There are times when you will have to be extremely patient with yourself; during that time you are still everything you are as a person, so do not use it as an opportunity to doubt yourself. Use this opportunity to love on yourself, not obsessively, but confidently with as much strength as possible in that circumstance. Trust yourself when you feel ready, not when you think or others think you should be ready.

Everyone lives with some degree of uncertainty, some of us more varying degrees than other; however, one thing you should attempt certainty of is yourself and your ability to move forward. You do not have to remain in any situation you dislike; there is always another option, only the limited resources we fear. Moving forward, away from people, away from a location, or away from a state of mind is okay. The best part is you can decide to be strong at any time; without an explanation, or excuse, or answer-unless you seek to provide it to yourself. You owe it to yourself to move forward, even if it involves inflicting the least amount of pain on others as possible. Every step you take or goal you set for yourself is supposed to be a step forward, and better than the last thing you did before. Come to grips with being hard on yourself if you are-while some people wallow in pity, maybe your self-criticism remains at a peak. Does pressure make you or break you? The way you treat yourself may work for you, and has been effective all this time. It's okay to push yourself to your full potential; however, you are not going to feel your absolute best every day. Technically, that would leave no room for improvement.

Knowing yourself will mean understanding yourself. Know who you are and no one can tell you who to be. It's important to stay in your realm-whatever you feel comfortable with; therefore there is no comparison to anyone else. If you are not careful people will require more out of you than what you are able to give or are willing to give, and address it as your own idea, the right idea, or attempting to inflict guilt for not fulfilling it. This is true for jobs, relationships, or anything or anyone that requires a commitment from you. Your temperament may require a bit of solitude and or isolation, to function on a daily or weekly basis. In the spiritual world, some zodiac signs require space as a part of their independence and individuality. Understand that loving yourself is a process that takes time. Over time our circumstances and experiences in life have molded us over and over, shaping us into who we are. Be careful what you let into your heart and into your mind- any and everything does not belong there; be emotionally intelligent. Your relationship with yourself should be resilient so that you can adapt as needed.

As religious people would have it, you already have all of the personal tools within yourself to do the things that you need or wish to do. We are not lacking if we are truly being ourselves. There is a void between what you need to do and want to do that needs attention-it needs to be filled. If there is ever something you wish to accomplish, you at least owe yourself the effort. Additionally, everything hard you've already been through or overcame has made you more and more resilient towards anything hard that is to come.

References

National Institute of Mental Health (2016). Anxiety Effects on Society Statistics. AnxietyCentre.com. Web. Retrieved September 1, 2016 from www.anxietycentre.com/anxiety-statistics-information.shtml

Breggin, P. R. (2014). Guilt Shame and Anxiety: understanding negative emotions.

Alcohol Rehab (2016). Alcohol Induced Anxiety. Alcoholrehab.com Web. Retrieved September 9, 2016 from http://alcoholrehab.com/alcoholism/alcohol-induced-anxiety/

Morris, C. E., Reiber, C., Roman, E. (2015). "Quantative Sex Differences in Response to the Dissolution of a Romantic Relationship". Binghampton University. *Evolutionary Behavioral Sciences* 9(4), 270-282. doi: 10.1037/EBS0000054

www.ingramcontent.com/pod-product-compliance
Lightning Source LLC
LaVergne TN
LVHW010031070426
835508LV00005B/291